A Collection of Poetry

Holly Parker

BookLeaf
Publishing

India | USA | UK

Presentation by *BookLeaf Publishing*

Web: www.bookleafpub.com

E-mail: info@bookleafpub.com

ISBN: 978-93-5744-447-7

First edition 2022

DEDICATION

To Ally, a friend who inspires, encourages and loves.

ACKNOWLEDGEMENT

I would like to acknowledge my lovely husband, who graciously steers me in the direction of creativity.

Loosening

We were made for touching skin,
Not to fear a warm breath,
But for belly-aching laughter
Echoing down hallways

Our hearts were made to be lit up
By the brightness in human eyes,
the harmless rivalry of friends,
And talking over the top of one another

Our souls were made to feel,
electrical pulses and sweaty skin,
Bright lights and glorious color,
To sing and sway and stomp

We were made for dimmed lights,
The whiskey-breath requests,
One hand on the piano,
The other conducting the room

We were made for dinner tables,
Legs entwined on sinking sofas,
Driving home through dark streets,
And for home to be our haven.

Hugs 'goodbye', dirty glasses,
empty plates and carpet crumbs;
These things, we were made for.

Garden

testing the earth beneath my feet
I survey the dusty surface
and gaps, like vivid veins, they creep
awaiting a refreshment.

my nozzle brings the drenching rains,
soaking deep into the cracks.
in a breath it quickly drains,
it cries for what it lacks.

I rake and sow, again I rake,
concern for each minuscule seed,
a forecast of what each will make,
of where each vine will lead.

one morn they rose into this world,
like a child from the unlit womb,
so I'll watch them all, growing proud,
cheering 'grow!' in full volume.

You Are My Life

You are my oxygen.
I'm 20 feet below
and finding your arms
is like breaking the surface.

You are my shelter.
What I run for in the rain,
the gentle pitter patter
of droplets against tin.

You are my fire.
warming my icy hands,
holding them in your own,
thawing me from the inside.

You are my stream.
Quenching all my thirst,
all the worries and woes,
reminding me to breathe.

You are my bread.
Giving me strength,
satisfying my nagging aches,
with blessed reassurance.

You are my life.

Diagnosis

I look, not for a magic cure,
for I am loved regardless
but, to be constantly unsure
it begs for diagnosis.

this in between, this thawing ice,
It's desolate and lonely.
to have an ear and sound advice!
to have somebody know me!

a closed, white door and fingers crossed,
I pray they'll see the signs
'please don't let my words be lost,
These traits are not benign!'

now out of breath, I need to know
Why must it be this way?
for the strain inside my heart, it grows
with every marring day.

The Snail

The snail recedes to the familiar darkness of its
coiled shell,
a homegrown haven to repel the soft, spring
showers.

It does not fear the big and brutal world beyond,
but takes its time, trudging the earthy surface
ever so leisurely.

The little creature has so much of it, time, that is.
Never late, never early, yet still, never rushing.

Leaving its mark of silver thread, it goes about
its day.
A curious life to envy.

Rustling Secrets

Age lines etched in bark,
Wise eyes peeking from hollows,
rustling secrets.

A Plea

A steady flow of helpless tears
What happened to the golden years?
I wither from unfounded fears,
Staring at the wall.

Is this the life God chose for me?
Shaping me like pottery
Ignoring my incessant plea
To take away this thorn.

My heart and spirit limp and sag
Every time that I'm alone
A voice inside speaks an endless nag
For each mistake I can't atone.

Bending down, I kneel to pray
Imagining a brighter day
When all the ghosts are blown away,
Walking pastures, green.

Sunday Morning

My fingertips wade through smoke-scented hair
- a reminder of yesterday's dusk,
stealing back moments we lost with cherished
company.
Now, you cloak my body with yours
and remind me what Sunday mornings are for,
clinging to this blissful rest, no longer in
abundance.
I welcome the glowing stripes seeping through,
escapees from a day clear and blue.
Naught but leisure to greet me peacefully
once I arise.

Pretty People

pretty people
sit in their pretty houses
so proud
so prosperous
a four sided, four walled
picture of perfection
peck peck pecking
at the metal plated door
are the powerless and poor
what a proper pity

Dice

six and one
live on opposite sides
of a planet-sized dice
they are both just black dots on white plastic,
made of the same thing
yet will never meet.
one will never know six intimately
and whilst six has so much more than one will
ever have,
They are both just black dots on white plastic.
and as this planet-sized cube
rolls around the board game of life
it will turn,
over and over and over ,
yet still, six and one will never meet,
six will never know one intimately,
six will never fathom how one lives their life
with six times less
or what it is like to be left behind in this
achingly slow board game of life.
stop.
PEEL THOSE BLACK DOTS OFF THAT
WHITE PLASTIC AND STEP BACK!
understand that,
the dice is not loaded,

we have no control over where it lands
or why,
in this irrepressible board game called life,
some sides have less black dots
than if they had the option to decide.
but,
and I think that some might not know
we are under no obligation to roll,
over and over and over
we are under no blind obligation,
to leave all our dot-shaped differences to chance
obliviously content on the white plastic face,
where our black dots land.

The Fields Where Flowers Grow

peaceful as the cotton-ball clouds above,
a place where people dance and fall in love,
are the fields where flowers grow

a place soft like cushions for the toes
where children forget all of their woes
are the fields where flowers grow

animals blissfully graze
men and women sing songs of praise
in the fields where flowers grow

gods tapestry of purples and pinks
detail as though drawn with ink
are the fields where flowers grow

thunderous

like the tiniest whisper
in a hushed library
so is my heart
when you're beside me -
thunderous.

Glitter Girl

somebody once told me that they'd truly found
the way
to brighten up your life and bring joy to
everyday life.
'sprinkle a little glitter on your hair and on your
face,
being careful not to leave it all over the place.'
so each day before the mirror, as I made myself
pristine,
I made sure to add some glitter as part of my
routine.
the compliments were flowing and my esteem
record high,
as long as I had glitter, surely I'd get by.
each day as I got ready, more glitter I would add
nobody had warned me too much glitter could
be bad!
cloaked in coats of glitter,
my face hidden to the world,
so I became known as

the glitter girl.

they promised I'd be happy,
and at first they had been right

but now glitter had taken over
my body, face and sight.
I thought I would find joy,
instead I've glitter in every wrinkle
I wish I'd took the warning
saying 'only use a sprinkle.'

A Newfound Home

sitting in a field of flowers,
We sat and spoke for hours and hours.
on checkered rugs we stretch our legs,
careless of the week ahead.
I ate soft cheese and strawberries
and let my hair flow in the breeze.
naked trees still yet to bloom,
made way for sun all afternoon.
and as we packed our things away,
I thanked God for this special day -
the shining sun, the peaceful tone,
gracious friends, and a new found home.

Clarity

clarity, where are you?
I saw you through a freshly cleaned window
back before the fog collapsed on the mountain.
I wondered if something so pure could be real.
my wonder turned to doubt and
suddenly you were gone.

clarity, where are you?
your presence is far more comfortable
than the clouds you hide behind.
don't be long gone now,
for you are dearly missed.

Rainbow Lenses

a child looks to the sky,
with rainbow lenses in their specs,
hopeful at the adventures to come,
free from all bitterness and vex.

their peer then searches for his specs too,
but reality looms like a dark, grey cloud
his specs were lost long ago,
no going back, no hope they'd be found.

maybe it's more true to say
of his rainbow lenses, rather,
they were not lost by the child's fault,
but stolen by another.

"but who", you ask, "would commit
such an indecent act?"
the suspects here are many,
so we must survey the facts.

Was it the absent father?
or the mother's sudden relapse?
the overbearing billboards?
or their jealousy perhaps?

nevertheless, these little people,
carry on with a skip and a smile,
they've lost their rainbow glasses,
but are resilient all the while.

Wheat and Weeds

orange plains turned purple
coating desert sands
mesmerizing, to those
unfamiliar with this land

but to the hardy farmer
with his cattle herd to feed
these vast and violet fields
are a filthy, violent weed

its beauty is deceptive
and whilst wheat cannot compare
one will be thrown to the fire
and one will have fruit to bear

Narrow or Wide?

narrow or wide?
two paths collide
here at a crossroad,
I'm called to decide -
narrow or wide?
the wide is coated with footprints
but as I look into the distance
I see... darkness.
narrow or wide?
the narrow is steep
and, whilst it's carried less feet,
afar a bright light seeps.
but how to get there?
I look at both roads and compare,
narrow or wide?
The wide is flat, picked by many for its ease.
The narrow is steep, by no means a breeze.
narrow or wide?
I decide,
with end goal in sight -
narrow.

At the End of the Rainbow

When will the bullies hide,
the shy stride,
and hate subside?
At the end of the rainbow?
When will we weep no more,
find the shore,
the silent roar?
At the end of the rainbow?
When will we drop our spears,
discard our fears,
embrace the years?
At the end of the rainbow?
Empty hope will but withhold,
the pot of gold,
for folklore told,
from pages, old,
of an endless rainbow.
Let hope fall on another mound,
where love abounds,
risen and crowned,
the true hope found,
in the promise of a rainbow.

A Loss So Abrupt

When did I ask
for help the last time?
Sleep in the dark
and was perfectly fine?

When did I start
counting the costs?
Walk through the market
without getting lost?

When was the choice
laid in my hands?
When did my voice
start making demands?

Did I lose track
or forget to look up?
Now I'll long and look back
at a loss so abrupt.

These Meadows Green

These meadows green
and grass pristine,
inclines steep and rolling,
down valleys, up hills
where cows stand still,
picturesque for strolling.

I rise and fall,
to pass it all
on wheels that know each turn,
glimpse left, peek right,
behold each sight
each morning and return.

9 789357 444477